# What is Shojo Beat?

*Shojo Beat* magazine and manga volumes feature the best of shojo manga, straight from Japan. The Shojo Beat line includes blockbuster titles like Matsuri Hino's *Vampire Knight,* and Arina Tanemura's *The Gentlemen's Alliance †,* Ai Yazawa's *NANA,* and Yuu Watase's *Absolute Boyfriend,* as well as fresh new stories such as Aya Nakahara's *Love★Com* and Aqua Mizuto's *Yume Kira Dream Shoppe.*

## Shojo Beat Magazine

This monthly magazine brings the best of Japanese manga (including six serialized titles!), style, culture, music and art to U.S. readers. Presented in the authentic right-to-left format, *Shojo Beat* magazine includes reader art and letters, contests, recipes, fashion tips, drawing how-tos and much more!

## Shojo Beat Manga

The Shojo Beat manga line brings the diverse creations of leading Japanese shojo manga artists to the United States in collected manga volume form. Shojo Beat manga presents pulse-quickening shojo in its original right-to-left format. Exquisitely drawn, these diverse tales of adventure, love and self-discovery, plus a host of compelling characters, are at the heart of each Shojo Beat manga title.

. . . . . . . . . . . . . . . . . . . . . . . . . . . . . . . . . . . . . . . . . . . . . . . . . . . . . . . .

D1282642

**Beat** MANGA FROM THE HEART

www.shojobeat.com

Project Manager **Carrie Shepherd**
Design **Frances O. Liddell**
Editor in Chief, Books **Alvin Lu**
Editor in Chief, Magazines **Marc Weidenbaum**
VP of Publishing Licensing **Rika Inouye**
VP of Sales **Gonzalo Ferreyra**
Sr. VP of Marketing **Liza Coppola**
Publisher **Hyoe Narita**

**HIGH SCHOOL DEBUT**
Story & Art **Kazune Kawahara**
Translation & Adaptation **Gemma Collinge**
Touch-up & Lettering **Mark Griffin**
Design **Izumi Hirayama**
Editor **Amy Yu**

**MONKEY HIGH!**
Story & Art **Shouko Akira**
Translation & Adaptation **Mai Ihara**
Touch-up & Lettering **John Hunt**
Design **Hidemi Dunn**
Editor **Amy Yu**

**MIXED VEGETABLES**
Story & Art **Ayumi Komura**
Translation **JN Productions**
English Adaptation **Stephanie VW Lucianovic**
Touch-up & Lettering **Gia Cam Luc**
Design **Yukiko Whitley**
Editor **Pancha Diaz**

**WE WERE THERE**
Story & Art **Yuki Obata**
Translation **Tetsuichiro Miyaki**
English Adaptation **Nancy Thistlethwaite**
Touch-up Art & Lettering **Inori Fukuda Trant**
Design **Izumi Hirayama**
Editor **Nancy Thistlethwaite**

**BLANK SLATE**
Story & Art **Aya Kanno**
Translation
**John Werry, HC Language Solutions, Inc.**
English Adaptation **Carla Sinclair**
Touch-up Art & Lettering **James Gaubatz**
Design **Sam Elzway**
Editor **Joel Enos**

**CAPTIVE HEARTS**
Story & Art **Matsuri Hino**
Translation & Adaptation **Andria Cheng**
Touch-up Art & Lettering **Sabrina Heep**
Design **Amy Martin**
Editor **Amy Yu**

Printed in the U.S.A.
Published by VIZ Media, LLC
P.O. Box 77010
San Francisco, CA 94107

## ——— EXPLANATION OF AGE RATINGS ———

**TEEN** Recommended for ages 13 and up. May contain violence, language, suggestive situations and alcohol or tobacco use.

ratings.viz.com

**OLDER TEEN** Recommended for ages 16 and up. May contain graphic violence, language, suggestive situations, brief nudity and alcohol or tobacco use.

ratings.viz.com

# CONTENTS

## Who doesn't need a love "coach" in high school?

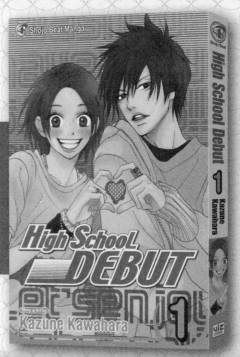

Back in junior high, Haruna Nagashima was only interested in two things: softball and manga. Now that she's starting high school, Haruna's focus has changed—she wants to snag a boyfriend and have the romance of her dreams!

**ABOUT THE CREATOR**

Kazune Kawahara is from Hokkaido prefecture in Japan and was born on March 11th (a Pisces!). She made her manga debut at age 18 with *Kare no Ichiban Sukina Hito* (His Most Favorite Person). Her other works include *Sensei!*, serialized in *Bessatsu Margaret* magazine. Her hobby is interior redecorating.

RATED T FOR TEEN
ratings.viz.com

High School Debut
ISBN-13: 978-1-4215-1481-9
Trim size: 5 x 7-1/2"
KOKO DEBUT © 2003 by Kazune Kawahara/SHUEISHA Inc.

CRACK

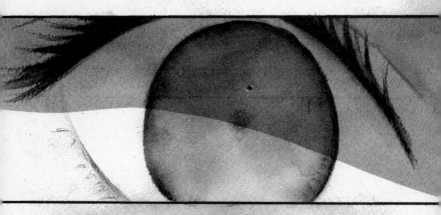

GOODBYE...

...SUMMER.

MEIRYOU

Yeah!

Come on!

Bring it!

...WAS A REALLY SPORTY GIRL UP UNTIL HIGH SCHOOL.

I PRACTICED LIKE CRAZY FROM MORNING TO NIGHT FOR THREE YEARS STRAIGHT.

You can't even field a ball like that? You klutz!

Run! Run till you drop!

I PUT ALL MY TIME INTO BEING AN ACE PITCHER FOR THE SCHOOL SOFTBALL TEAM.

I ALSO MADE SOME GREAT FRIENDS.

I GAVE IT MY ALL, AND I REALLY ENJOYED MYSELF.

BUT...

...THERE WAS SOMETHING ELSE...

THE JOY OF VICTORY MADE THE PAIN OF PRACTICE WORTH IT.

BUT I FOUND OUT I WAS WRONG.

I THOUGHT EVERYONE AUTOMATICALLY GOT A BOYFRIEND WHEN THEY WENT TO HIGH SCHOOL.

MY FIRST SEMESTER.

"Wear two pendants to make guys notice you." Hm.

Oh, Haruna! Studying hard again, I see?

"This season's hottest outfit!" I see!

AFTER TRYING MY BEST...

I REALIZED THAT I'D HAVE TO WORK HARD AT IT.

CHECK IT OUT!

THAT GIRL'S SO FAMOUS NOW!

...I WAS NOW JUST WAITING...

...TO GET HIT ON FOR THE FIRST TIME IN MY LIFE.

...THAT OPPORTUNITIES DON'T JUST COME ALONG EVERY DAY.

CRASH

OW... OUCH...

THAT'S RIGHT, HUH.

I ALSO KNOW FROM EXPERIENCE THAT OPPORTUNITIES...

HOW ABOUT LOOKING FOR ANOTHER COACH?

LOOKS LIKE I'LL JUST HAVE TO STICK WITH SELF-STUDY.

...DON'T ALWAYS END IN SUCCESS.

NO...

I'LL ONLY TRY AGAIN IF I MEET SOMEONE ELSE THAT MY HEART TELLS ME IS RIGHT...

HUH.

OH...

...SHE WENT TO GO GET A DRINK.

HEY.

WHERE'S ASAMI?

HOT CLOTHING!

SEXY HAIR!

MUST-HAVE FRAGRANCES

IS THERE SOMETHING YOU WANNA SAY? C'MON! SPIT IT OUT!

...

...HURT PEOPLE"...

IF SOMEONE YOU LOVED SAID THAT ABOUT YOU...

I WONDER IF SOMEONE HE DATED SAID THAT.

WHAT'S WITH THOSE SAD EYES?!

...THAT WOULD BE PRETTY HARSH.

SQUEAK

OH, WHAT-EVER.

WAIT...

...YOH!

...

**FIND LOVE USING FENG...**

PRETTY IN PINK!

PINK

I'M POSITIVE...

...I PERFECTED MY LOOK TODAY.

I RE-SEARCHED FOR HOURS AND PUT TOGETHER EVERYTHING THAT'S HOT RIGHT NOW.

ALL GUYS DIG DRESSES! WE ASKE REAL GU

BE LOVED WITHOUT A DOU

BE SEXY WITH

SO...

...IF THIS DOESN'T WORK...

...I DON'T KNOW WHAT ELSE I CAN DO.

# Going bananas for love!

Haruna Aizawa thinks that school life is just like a monkey mountain—all the monkeys form cliques, get into fights, and get back together again. The school that she just transferred to is no exception. There's even a boy called Macharu Yamashita who reminds her of a baby monkey!

## ABOUT THE CREATOR

Shouko Akira made her debut in 1995 with *Taiyo-kei ha Kimi no Mono* (*The Solar System Is Yours*), which was serialized in Japan's *Deluxe Bessatsu Shojo Comic*. She is also the author of *Times Two*, a collection of five romantic short stories that's available from VIZ MEDIA.

Monkey High!
ISBN-13: 978-1-4215-1518-2
Trim size: 5 x 7-1/2"

1ST
MONKEY

MISS CONTRARY VS.

IS THIS A...

...BABY MONKEY?

THANKS TO THE CORRUPTION SCANDAL MY FATHER WAS INVOLVED IN AS A POLITICIAN...

...THE KISS-UPS AT MY OLD SCHOOL CHANGED THEIR TUNE OVERNIGHT.

I DIDN'T TELL YOU TO PROMOTE YOURSELF!

SMACK

Ow!

Whatever. Get out of here.

...IT'S FINE.

I'M SO SORRY ABOUT THAT.

They're a rowdy bunch.

YEAH...I GUESS THINGS ARE JUST SO CRAZY...

IT'S NOT LIKE SHE REALLY HAS A CHOICE...

I HEARD HARUNA'S TRANSFERRING.

NOT THAT I CARE.

EVER SINCE THAT FIRST DAY...

...ALL THE GIRLS HATE ME, APPARENTLY.

THAT'S WHAT YOU GET FOR TAPPING A POLITICIAN'S DAUGHTER.

No kidding

NOW I CAN'T EVEN INTRODUCE HER TO MY PARENTS.

THIS SUCKS, MAN...

IT'S NOT LIKE YOU CAN LET YOUR GUARD DOWN...

...JUST BECAUSE YOU THINK YOU'RE IN A GROUP...

THAT'S MY COSTUME!

HEY.

THANKS!

WOW!

YEAH.

REALLY?!

IT WON'T TAKE LONG TO FIX THIS.

DON'T WORRY ABOUT IT.

HIGH SCHOOL BOYS...

...SHOULDN'T SMILE WITH SUCH SINCERITY...

SEEMS LIKE YOU'RE PRETTY INTO YOUR ROLE.

OH YEAH.

About that...

Dwarf...

Home Economics!

HE BEAT ME TO IT...

NICE.

THANKS.

I ACTUALLY WANTED TO ADJUST THE SIZE...

SURE!

I'M ABLE TO PUT IT ON, BUT...

SHUP

...THE NECK AND ARMS ARE KINDA TIGHT.

Muffle

DON'T LAUGH!!

IT'S PERFECT!

Though he looks more like a clown than a dwarf...

Ha ha ha

SORRY.

HOLD STILL. I'M MARKING IT RIGHT...

YOU CAN FIX IT?

I THOUGHT THE PATTERN WAS A LITTLE SMALL...

All the other dwarves are girls.

The shoes are his own.

WHAT'S THAT!

... MAYBE.

HAHA!

MAYBE
THAT'S
WHY...

...I
FEEL
TINGLY...

HIS
HAIR...

...IS
BRUSHING
MINE...

SLAM

SHE'S ...

SHE'S FIXING MY COSTUME...

YOU TWO!

WHAT ARE YOU TWO DOING?!

HOW SUSPICIOUS! THE TWO OF YOU ALL ALONE TOGETHER!

SO IT'S A GENERAL CONSENSUS THAT HE'S A BABY MONKEY...

...BUT HE CAN TRANSFORM INTO A DOG.

HE MAY LOOK LIKE A BABY MONKEY...

Look who's talking!

MEN ARE DOGS. YOU SHOULD KNOW THAT.

HARUNA...

WHAT ABOUT PRACTICE?

HEY.

THIS IS SNOW WHITE'S COSTUME.

THEY'RE FIGHTING OVER THE SCENE WITH THE HUNTER AND THE PEDDLER.

BUT IT LOOKS LIKE YOU'VE TRANSFORMED INTO A DWARF TODAY!

HMM?

Feel my dwarf wrath!

KICK

WHA...

WHATEVER, ATSU. YOU'RE TOTALLY FALLING FOR HER TRICKS.

LET'S ALL CALM DOWN!

I ASKED HER TO DO IT AS A JOKE.

PUTTING ON SOMEONE ELSE'S COSTUME LIKE THAT!

WHAT DO YOU THINK YOU'RE DOING?!

YOU PROBABLY HAD YOUR EYE ON HIM FROM THE BEGINNING, DIDN'T YOU?

EXACTLY. SHE'S JUST PLAYING YOU.

SORRY.

You're right.

NO NEED TO APOLOGIZE...

WHERE DO YOU THINK YOU ARE?

LOOKING ON FROM THE TOP?

OR ARE YOU JUST AN OUTSIDE OBSERVER?

HOW AM I SUPPOSED TO KNOW!

WHO CARES!

WHY DID HE HAVE TO LOOK AT ME LIKE THAT?

WHAT'S HIS PROBLEM?

HE'S ALWAYS LAUGHING LIKE A FOOL...

...ALWAYS LAUGHING...

PEOPLE OUTSIDE THE CLUB CAN'T COME IN HERE.

CLICK

SO WHO IS HE?

RIGHT...

HE'S FROM MY OLD SCHOOL.

MY EX.

AS TO WHAT
EXACTLY
HAPPENED...

I'M NOT REALLY SURE MYSELF...

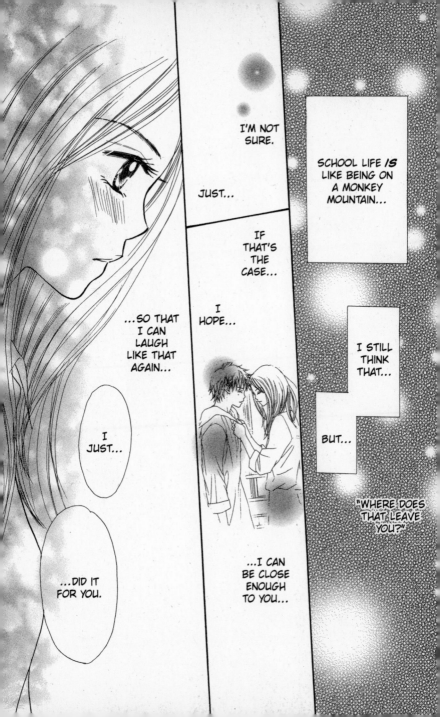

I'M NOT SURE.

JUST...

SCHOOL LIFE *IS* LIKE BEING ON A MONKEY MOUNTAIN...

IF THAT'S THE CASE...

...SO THAT I CAN LAUGH LIKE THAT AGAIN...

I HOPE...

I STILL THINK THAT...

I JUST...

BUT...

..I CAN BE CLOSE ENOUGH TO YOU...

"WHERE DOES THAT LEAVE YOU?"

...DID IT FOR YOU.

*Can Hanayu create the recipe for happiness?*

Hanayu Ashitaba is the daughter of the celebrated Patisserie Ashitaba, but all she wants to do is be a sushi chef. Hayato Hyuga is the son of the prestigious Sushi Hyuga, and all he wants to do is be a pastry chef! It's love and leftovers at Oikawa High School Cooking Department as these star-crossed gourmands do their best to reach their cuisine dreams!

## ABOUT THE CREATOR

Ayumi Komura was born a Capricorn in Kagoshima Prefecture. Her favorite number is 22, and her hobbies include watching baseball. Her previous title is *Hybrid Berry*, about a high school girl who ends up posing as a boy on her school's baseball team.

SO, YOU'RE THE DAUGHTER OF A PASTRY CHEF, YET YOU CAN FILLET A FISH LIKE THAT—IT'S AMAZING!

I MEAN, YOUR FAMILY RUNS A PASTRY SHOP, RIGHT?

YEAH...

WELL, HYUGA...

I GUESS YOU EXPECT ME TO SAY, "YOU'RE THE SON OF A SUSHI CHEF, YET YOU CAN BAKE WELL—IT'S AMAZING!"

GULP

*That's his reaction.*

BO—ING!

*This was supposed to be a dorayaki!*
←

I WAS PROUD THAT MY FAMILY HAD A PASTRY SHOP.

YOU'RE SO LUCKY, HANA.

I WISH MY FAMILY OWNED A PASTRY SHOP.

...AND HE LOOKED SO COOL.

MY FATHER MADE SUCH PRETTY CAKES...

BUT ONE DAY...

MOM'S GONE OUT...

...SO IT'S JUST THE TWO OF US FOR DINNER TONIGHT.

The prep's all done.

Both father and daughter wear black to the sushi shop.

That's because you might get soy sauce on your shirt.

Please don't you spill on your shirt.

Huh?

MOM, CAN YOU BUY FISH TODAY?

BUT...

HUH?!

ASHITABA

I'LL HELP YOU.

Fish have scary eyes, don't you think?

BUT...

I PRETENDED THAT I WAS HELPING MOM JUST BECAUSE SHE DIDN'T LIKE FISH.

BUT THE MOMENT I TOUCHED A FISH THAT FIRST TIME...

**_The award-winning series known in Japan as Bokura ga Ita._**

Nanami Takahashi falls for Motoharu Yano, the most popular, carefree boy in class. For Nanami, it's first love, but Yano is still grieving the death of his girlfriend who died the year before.

### ABOUT THE CREATOR

Yuki Obata's birthday is January 9. Her debut manga, *Raindrops*, won the Shogakukan Shinjin Comics Taisho Kasaku Award in 1998. Her current series, *We Were There* (Bokura ga Ita), won the 50th Shogakukan Manga Award and was adapted into an animated television series. She likes sweets, coffee, drinking with friends and scary stories. Her hobby is browsing in bookshops.

RATED
T+
FOR OLDER TEEN
ratings.viz.com

We Were There
ISBN-13: 978-1-4215-2018-6
Trim size: 5 x 7-1/2"
Bokura ga Ita © Yuuki OBATA/Shogakukan Inc.

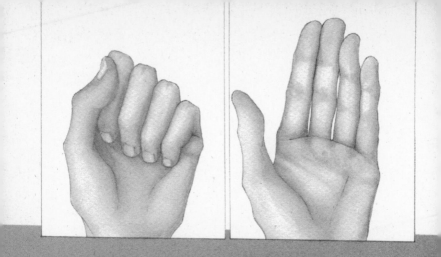

AT THE TIME, HE WAS 15 YEARS OLD.

AND NOW, HE'S ONLY 16.

BUT THE REALITY HE MUST FACE...

...IS FAR GREATER THAN YOUTH WILL ALLOW.

# We Were There

# Chapter 1

swnk

MY SECOND DAY OF HIGH SCHOOL...

I'M NANAMI TAKAHASHI. I'M 15.

I DON'T WANT YOU TO BE LATE FOR SCHOOL THIS EARLY ON, OKAY?

NANAMI!

AREN'T YOU READY YET?

SO MANY PRINTOUTS AND SYLLABUSES...

A NEW CLASS-ROOM...

TEXTBOOKS WITH STIFF BINDINGS...

WHAT IS THIS?!

THESE ARE REALLY HARD.

MAYBE I'M STUPID...?

Math I

I'VE NEVER REALLY LIKED SPRING, THE START OF THE NEW SCHOOL YEAR.

ARE YOU ON YOUR WAY TO HOME EC?

YOU MIND IF I JOIN YOU?

WHICH MIDDLE SCHOOL DID YOU GO TO?

CALL ME NANA.

NANA !!

TAKAHASHI-SAN?

YAY! SHE REMEM-BERS ME FROM CLASS!!

YEAH!

HUH?

YOU SIT IN THE FRONT ROW, RIGHT?

MINAMI.

WE WENT TO NISHI.

I'M NANAMI TAKA-HASHI!!

HA HA HA

SCORE! ♡

NO WAY.

I'M SO HAPPY.

THEY SEEM NICE.

THEN WE CAN ASK HER.

?

ASK HER WHAT?

SHE SITS NEXT TO ME.

YAMAMOTO-SAN WENT THERE.

OH!

THERE AREN'T ANY GIRLS FROM ASAHI IN OUR CLASS, ARE THERE?

WE HAD A CLASS WITH MOTOHARU LAST WINTER.

WHO?

ABOUT MOTOHARU.

AND NOW WE'RE IN THE SAME HOMEROOM!

HA HA HA

WE'RE SO EXCITED!

BUT HE'S SUPER-POPULAR.

I WOULDN'T CALL HIM THAT...

He's not the cute type either.

OH.

REALLY?

HE MUST BE GOOD-LOOKING.

THERE WAS A BOY LIKE THAT AT MY MIDDLE SCHOOL.

HE HAD FOUR OR FIVE FANS IN EVERY CLASS.

HA HA HA HA

...YOUNG AND OLD.

I DIDN'T REALIZE THERE WAS A GUY LIKE THAT IN MY CLASS.

ANYWAY, HE'S POPULAR WITH BOTH GIRLS AND BOYS...

EVERYONE CALLS HIM MOTOHARU.

BUT FOR MOTO-HARU...

I wasn't interested in him, though.

I WAS TOO NERVOUS YESTERDAY TO NOTICE MUCH.

THIS MAY SEEM CRAZY, BUT...

Fwaah ...

...EVEN THOUGH I DIDN'T ASK HIS NAME...

...I KNEW...

AH!

THANK YOU.

YOU'RE WEL-COME.

OH.

HA HA HA

YOU CAN BE THE CLASS PRESIDENT.

...

...EXACTLY WHO HE WAS.

HR

Tuesday, April 9th

Day Duty

Abe
Ishii

MOTOHARU YANO.

DID YOU MEAN MIZUGUCHI-SAN?

WHO IS THAT?

HUH?

WHAT?

WHO?

...

MIZU-HARA?

HEH

gloom

HA HA

PBFFT!

...

BA HA HA

THAT'S BAD...

No way!

SHE DOESN'T EVEN KNOW HER NAME.

AAAH! WHY ME?!

DID HE JUST LAUGH?!

...LET'S DETERMINE OUR GOAL FOR THE FIRST SEMESTER.

OKAY...

SO NOW...

DAMN YOU!

SHE WAS NOMINATED FOR PRESIDENT WHILE EVERYONE WAS MAKING FUN OF HER.

I COULD HEAR YOU LAUGHING.

SO...

SO?

I DON'T...

HE'S BAD NEWS.

...KIND OF...

SO...

...THAT'S ALL.

THIS GUY...

...SCARES ME.

Look!

...LIKE HIM.

YANO'S BENTO...

HEE HEE

...HAS THOSE BUNNY APPLES IN IT.

HOW CUTE!

MATH LOOKS REALLY HARD THIS YEAR.

I WONDER WHAT HIS LAST NAME WAS.

HMM.

SOMEONE TOLD ME HE HAD A DIFFERENT LAST NAME IN GRADE SCHOOL.

I THINK SO.

OH.

BUT I HEARD HIS PARENTS ARE DIVORCED.

IS YANO-KUN AN ONLY CHILD?

LET'S ASK YAMAMOTO-SAN ABOUT HIM.

WELL, I DON'T REALLY KNOW. IT'S JUST A RUMOR.

YOU SURE?

EVEN OLDER GIRLS.

I'M NOT TOO FOND OF JAPANESE CLASS EITHER.

...HE'S GONE OUT WITH LOTS OF GIRLS.

I HEARD THAT...

HAS HE BEEN DATING ANYONE?

LOOKS LIKE...

...I'M IN THE ONE-THIRD MINORITY.

I LIKE...

...ENGLISH, THOUGH.

...

...

...

...

...

IT'S NONE OF MY BUSINESS.

HOW WOULD I KNOW?

TO FIND OUT HOW TO BUY THE FULL VOLUME, VISIT WWW.VIZ.COM.

# Search your soul...or die trying!

What does it take to find your true inner self? Zen's memory has been wiped, and he can't remember if he's a killer or a hero. And a lot of people will do anything they can to keep it that way.

## ABOUT THE CREATOR

Aya Kanno was born in Tokyo, Japan. She is the creator of *Soul Rescue*, which has been published in the United States, and her latest work, *Otomen*, is currently being serialized in Japan's *BetsuHana* magazine. *Blank Slate* was originally published as *Akusaga* in Japan in *Hana to Yume* magazine.

The story of a man...

YEAH... WE FINALLY FOUND HIM.

IN THIS TOWN?

ARE YOU SURE?

IT SEEMS LIKE NO ONE HAS NOTICED BECAUSE ALMOST NO ONE KNOWS WHAT HE LOOKS LIKE.

IT'S MUCH BETTER THAN SULLYING MY NAME BY BEING A CRIMINAL, BUT I...

...DIDN'T PARTICULARLY CHOOSE THIS PATH FOR THE MONEY.

WANTED

EVER SINCE HE ALMOST KILLED ME YEARS AGO I'VE NEVER FORGOTTEN.

THOSE DARK DEMONIC EYES...

MORE CRIMES THAN EVEN THE GOVERNMENT KNOWS.

MURDER, ROBBERY, ASSAULT AND BATTERY... HE'S COMMITTED EVERY CRIME IMAGINABLE.

HE'LL BE MY BIGGEST HIT SO FAR.

HE'S KNOWN AS *ZEN*...

*DEAD OR ALIVE.* HE'S AN ULTRA A-CLASS TARGET.

I'LL PUT A STOP TO HIM.

KILLING HIM WILL BE WORTH-WHILE...

A PERSON HASN'T LIVED UNTIL THEY'VE *CONTROLLED* SOMEONE ELSE'S FATE... YOU KNOW WHAT I MEAN?

THAT'S WHY I NEED TO *CONTROL* HIM.

I'VE HEARD THAT YOU'RE SKILLED...

...BUT ZEN'S NOT YOUR AVERAGE THUG.

IF YOU STEAL SOMEONE'S LIFE, THAT PERSON'S CONSCIOUSNESS AND FUTURE...

YOU STEAL IT ALL.

THAT'S WHY BEING A BOUNTY HUNTER WHO CAN BUMP PEOPLE OFF LEGALLY...

...

THE HIGHEST LEVEL OF CONTROL IS DEALING DEATH.

I...

...SEEK ABSOLUTE *CONTROL*.

YOU'RE MY PLAYMATE TODAY?

...SINCE HE SO OPENLY REVEALS HIS NAME AND IS A PROSTITUTE.

...THEN CERTAINLY NO ONE WOULD THINK IT...

IF HE IS THE REAL THING...

THIS IS HIM?

THIS GUY, AS SLENDER AS A WOMAN, WITH DELICATE FEATURES TO MATCH, IS *THE* ZEN?

WHY ARE YOU DOING THIS?

YOU...

BUT STILL...

EVEN IF THIS GUY IS THE REAL ZEN, THERE'S NO WAY I CAN KILL HIM *HERE*.

...

I'M NOT WORKING PER SE.

FIRST I NEED TO GET CLOSE TO THE TARGET AND GET HIM TO LET DOWN HIS GUARD.

BECAUSE EVEN THE UNDERWORLD HAS RULES.

PEOPLE JUST COME AS THEY PLEASE, AND IF THEY CATCH MY INTEREST I FOOL AROUND WITH 'EM.

...IT WON'T BE LONG BEFORE THIS PLACE...

...GETS OLD TOO.

A GUN...

BUT...

?!

THIS MAN IS WITHOUT A DOUBT...

JOIN ME.

# 1

It's nice to meet you...

Or...hello.

This is Aya Kanno.

First of all, I need to apologize for something. Those of you who read *Blank Slate* when it was running in the magazine may have already noticed, but the Chapter 1 from that time has not been included in this graphic novel. Instead, Chapter 4 of the bonus episodes has been included as Chapter 1. This isn't a mistake, it was something I wanted. I'm terribly sorry to those of you who read the magazine, but I hope you will understand... I'll talk about why I did this in the next sidebar.

...

NOW WE WON'T HAVE ANY MONEY.

IF OUR MONEY RUNS OUT, WE'LL STEAL SOME MORE.

THERE'S NO NEED TO GET A ROOM IN A FIVE-STAR HOTEL JUST TO SLEEP...

...WHETHER IT'S PEOPLE OR THINGS.

ANYTHING GETS IN THE WAY, WE'LL DESTROY IT...

HE'S OUT OF CONTROL.

HE STARTED THINKING OF ME AS A COMPANION LONG AGO.

ARE YOU A CUSTOMER?

...KILL ZEN...

DON'T MOVE.

I CAN DO IT.

HE'S SURE TO HAVE COMPLETELY LET HIS GUARD DOWN.

THAT'S RIGHT.

KSHAK

NOW!

DO EXACTLY AS I SAY.

THAT'S RIGHT.

BUT WHAT ABOUT TOGETHER WITH AN INFAMOUS BOUNTY HUNTER?

HE'S NOT SOMEONE YOU CAN HANDLE.

...

LEAVE GETTING RID OF HIM TO ME.

I'VE GOT A GRUDGE AGAINST HIM.

...YOU'VE BEEN PRETENDING TO BE HIS ALLY, RIGHT?

TO GET HIM TO TRUST YOU...

...

RUSSO!

SHOOT.

...I WOULD HAVE KILLED HIM.

AS LONG AS YOU, HIS PARTNER, ARE IN FRONT OF ME, HE WON'T SHOOT ME.

EVEN WITHOUT YOUR HELP...

TO ME...

IS THAT TRUE?

BESIDES, HE CERTAINLY DOESN'T EXPECT YOU TO SHOOT HIM.

I WAS RAISED IN A WEALTHY HOUSEHOLD AND NEVER NEEDED ANYTHING...

...NEVER BEEN ANYTHING BUT TARGETS FOR CONTROL.

...OTHERS HAVE NEVER...

WHEN I WAS A KID I ENJOYED STEPPING ON ANTS.

AND I STILL FEEL THE SAME WAY.

OTHERS WERE BENEATH ME.

NOTHING BUT BORING AND WORTHLESS PEOPLE.

# A charming romance from the creator of Vampire Knight!

Carefree Megumi Kuroishi was living a life of luxury until the day a girl named Suzuka Kogami walked into his life. All of a sudden, Megumi finds himself kneeling at Suzuka's feet and prostrating himself like a servant! What Megumi doesn't know (until that very moment anyway) is that his family is cursed to follow the orders of the Kogami family.

## ABOUT THE CREATOR

Matsuri Hino burst onto the manga scene with her title *Kono Yume ga Sametara* (*When This Dream Is Over*), which was published in *LaLa DX* magazine. Hino was a manga artist a mere nine months after she decided to become one.

With the success of her popular series *Toraware no Minoue* (*Captive Hearts*), and *MeruPuri*, Hino has established herself as a major player in the world of shojo manga. *Vampire Knight* is currently serialized in *LaLa* in Japan and *Shojo Beat* magazines.

I SAY "WORKED"— PAST TENSE— FOR A REASON.

THREE YEARS AFTER SUZUKA WAS BORN, THE KOGAMI FAMILY...

...WENT MISSING DURING A TRIP TO CHINA.

TWELVE YEARS LATER, IT WAS DECLARED THEY HAD DIED IN AN ACCIDENT, AND THE MASTER'S WILL WAS OPENED...

MASTER...

I AM UNWORTHY OF SUCH PRAISE.

Sniff...

I AM TRULY HAPPY TO HAVE SERVED AS YOUR BUTLER.

KURO-ISHI...

YOU'VE HELPED US SO MUCH...

THANK YOU.

MY FATHER...

...AS A BUTLER.

...JUST AS OUR ANCESTORS HAD FOR GENERATIONS, WORKED FOR THE KOGAMI FAMILY...

PFFFT

Megumi, you won't believe this!!!

BANG

HM... THE TEA IS DELICIOUS TODAY...

WHAT'S WRONG WITH THAT?

I'VE BEEN STUDYING, YOU KNOW.

Ah!

YOU REALLY ENJOY DOING NOTHING, DON'T YOU?

YOU'RE LAZING AROUND AGAIN!

Master and his family have been found!!

YOU WON'T BELIEVE THIS, MEGUMI!!

WHAT IS IT?

OH, THAT'S RIGHT!

WH—

Emotional

AH... YES...

WHAT...?

I'M SURE MISS SUZUKA - HAS GROWN UP TO BE QUITE BEAUTIFUL.

YOU'LL SOON FIND OUT MORE ABOUT THE KUROISHI FATE FOR YOURSELF...

HEH

SHIVER

BA ZOOM

SIGH... GOOD-BYE, MY FUTURE FORTUNE...

I'M ON MY WAY TO CHINA RIGHT NOW TO COME GET YOU!!

...

IF YOU WERE SAFE, WHY DIDN'T YOU CONTACT US EARLIER ?!

OH, MASTER!

NOW THAT I HAVE NO MONEY, THERE ARE ONLY THREE CHOICES LEFT—GET A PART-TIME JOB SOMEWHERE...

WORK PART-TIME AT THIS MANSION...

DING DONG

OR...

GRIN

Master and his family died of a sudden illness 12 years ago in a rural part of China...

SOB SOB SOB SOB

CREAK

...KICK THE KOGAMI FAMILY OUT OF THIS HOUSE.

SNFF

I HAD NOTHING TO WORRY ABOUT AFTER ALL! ♡

Life of comfort, here I come! (Again!)

fantasies

sob sob sob

WELL, THEN!

IT BEGAN LONG AGO, DURING THE MUROMACHI ERA...

...WHEN THE INFAMOUS THIEF CALLED "KURONEKO-MARU"...

...SNUCK INTO A SAMURAI'S HOUSE...

...AND STOLE THE FAMILY'S HEIRLOOM, "THE SCROLL OF THE RISING DRAGON."

AFTER ARRIVING HOME WITH THE SCROLL, KURONEKO-MARU QUICKLY OPENED IT.

AND THEN...

A DRAGON GOD, THE GUARDIAN OF THE FAMILY, APPEARED...

...AND PUT A CURSE UPON KURONEKO-MARU'S DESCENDANTS FOR A HUNDRED GENERATIONS.

I HAVE TO RUN AWAY...

FU QIN ...*

*Chinese for "father."

HUH?

THAT'S THE LIBRARY, ISN'T IT?

PAPA ...

MAMA ...

SHE MUST BE SO LONELY ...

WHEN MISS SUZUKA WAS FIVE, BOTH OF HER PARENTS DIED...

THAT'S RIGHT...

# Turn Back the Clock

In the 30th century, Kyoko Suomi is the princess of Earth—but she wants absolutely nothing to do with the throne! In order to get out of her royal responsibilities, she'll have to travel through time to find her long-lost twin. Will Kyoko locate her missing sister, or will she end up as Earth's reluctant ruler?

Find out in *Time Stranger Kyoko*—manga on sale now!

# Time Stranger Kyoko

**By Arina Tanemura,**
creator of *Full Moon,*
*The Gentlemen's Alliance†*
and *I•O•N*

# Shojo Beat™

MANGA from the HEART

## The Shojo Manga Authority

The most **ADDICTIVE** shojo manga stories from Japan **PLUS** unique editorial coverage on the arts, music, culture, fashion, and much more!

12 GIANT issues for ONLY $34.99*

That's 51% OFF the cover price!